MW01516449

Gardener At Heart

To Susan —
Enjoy!
Jane Gibson

Jane Gibson

July 17, 2016

Published by Jane Gibson.
Printed by CreateSpace, an Amazon.com company.
ISBN: 978-1-5121-1819-3

The reference used for the scientific names for flowers is Russ Jolley's *Wildflowers of the Columbia River Gorge,* 1988. Some scientific names have been changed since then, but the older names have been retained here so that these flowers can be looked up in already-published reference books. Scientific names have not been used for plants whose common names are well-known and unambiguous. Any errors are my own.

To my husband and children with love.

And to my friends in Last Thursday Writer's Group with thanks.

Table Of Contents

Book One

Book Two

Index Of Titles And First Lines

Book One

Garden Habitat

Come on!
Go wild with me!
Let's root up carrots,
graze on lettuce,
bite a tomato off the vine.
Come on!
The corn is tall enough to hide us.
On far-off hills,
the deer approve.

Seed People

The seed people wait
Wrapped in blankets
Brown and black
They wait
Humming
Heads hidden
Here an eye shows
They wait
Till earth's kiss
Circling sun
Bid them come
Hit their drums
Slip off brown and black
Show their new dance clothes—
Wait!
Didn't they wear those
Last year?

A Lady Reposes (Mountain Lady's Slipper, *Cypripedium montanum*)

Her bedroom's full of shrubs and oaks;
Amid the prickly undergrowths
She's cleared a space and made her bed
And sat down in her petticoats.

Her hat, her coat, her gloves, all shed,
Her dress unbuttoned on the bed;
Like russet leaves she's let them fall,
And stretched, and yawned, and scratched her head.

The dappling sun is hot and tall.
A napping bird gives out a call.
She fluffs her silken underclothes;
She pats her skirts and drapes her shawl.

At last she lifts a slippered toe
And with a tug undoes the bow;
The ribbon's in a knot, and so
She goes to sleep, and lets it go.

Field Guide (Ponderosa Pine)

I took my key, I stood outside,
    I looked up at the sky;
I could not count the needles, they
    were growing way too high.
I scrutinized the bark instead—
    I looked it in the eye.

I broke some puzzle pieces off
    that giant scratchy chest,
And right there underneath I found
    the color of the west—
The very stuff the robin surely
    uses on its vest.

The bark was split by canyons,
    every one of them was grand;
Some insects were exploring in
    this horizontal land,
And one set out to study my
    mysterious giant hand.

I pressed my ear against the bark
    where nothing crawled around;
The wind was in the needles, and
    I heard a hissing sound;
I heard the big bole flexing from
    the tip down to the ground.

I looked straight up the trunk again;
    the clouds were going fast,
And for one dizzy moment there
    the tree became a mast
And I was riding Earth somewhere—
    and then the moment passed.

The wind got stronger, and it must
    have snapped a branch-tip free;
I saw it fall, as if the tree
    had tossed it down to me;
I picked it up and counted, and
    I looked into my key.

I crushed some needles and they smelled
    so potent and so clean;
I found the page and learned the name—
    the drawing there was keen—
And now they grow all over, where
    before it was just green.

Grass Widows Near Horsethief Butte

Some people say heaven's up there
But I say earth's the miracle place
I say this dark rocky swell of dirt
Is where spirits dwell
The flowing turf is clouds of glory
These slender leaves are anchored angels
These blowing purple bells are unfurled wings
And I say, I believe, I believe.

Chat With A Fly Fisherman
(Narrow-Leaf Paintbrush,
Orthocarpus attenuatus)

My bigger brothers love to paint;
With two-three colors they'll create
A scene that could have brought Monet to give them lilies up.

But I'm a fisherman myself;
When spring is high there's nothing else
I'd rather do than cast my twelve-foot leader on the breeze.

My rod is lean, my tackle light;
Up close my fly's a marvelous sight:
I always tie the hackle white with eye-beads tilting up.

I cast a forward rolling loop—
At last my quarry stalls and stoops—
If only I can set the hook I'll bring you to your knees.

Draba verna Speaks

They call me *Draba verna,* and I think
I've figured out just what that means, although
I don't know Greek or Latin. Yes, I think
I know. I'm sure they've seen that in full blow
My flower's as big and bright as my whole self,
Which, sometimes green and sometimes brilliant red,
Will thrive and multiply where nothing else
Will grow, a silver lining to the lead
Of many feet. On stony ground I bring
The clouds to earth, like mountain lambs at play;
I know the song of many a secret thing,
And lay out galaxies upon the clay.
    Those names must surely signify that I
    Am big at heart, big as the open sky.

The Old Stargazer (Old-Growth Grand Fir)

At night I watch the pageant of the stars,
And bit by bit I learn their lofty ways;
Atop my tower I observe afar
Bright skaters gliding round the pond of space.
At times when rowdy clouds obscure the show,
I pace and growl, impatient with delay;
At times some small commotion down below
Disturbs my daily doze, and bids me say
Hello to all my brothers. Ah, but then
Earth rolls, and kicks her flukes, and all her space
Is filled with phosphorescence once again,
And I see nothing else. These are my ways:
    To learn, to ponder, and to feast my eyes
    On all the radiant splendors of the skies.

The Farm Wife (East-Side White Oak, *Quercus garryana*)

Some folks don't really like this place,
This hard old rocky hillside farm,
But this is where we've settled down,
And we don't do too bad, I guess.
We make a living, anyway,
With what we have right here and now,
And that's more than some folks can say.
I've got a real nice sunrise view,
And there's a fair amount of birds.
I keep my feeders full for them;
I go out early every day,
No matter what the weather is.
The moths are really something, too.
I must have seen a hundred kinds.
Why, who'd have thought that brown on brown
Could come so many different ways?
We like to sit outside to hear
The little frogs that sometimes call,
And later on the owls are close,
And once we saw a cougar track.
I've seen a lot of things from here.
I've lived my whole life in this spot
And raised my children best I could.
They all live right here on this hill,
All just a jump and yell away.
I've never really felt the need

For liberation like some do.
My life has always seemed to ask
My best and then a little more.
I may not look like much to you.
Depends on how you look, I guess.
You'll have to take me as I am
And find what good you can.

The Old-Timer (Common Mullein, *Verbascum thapsus*)

Well, I was born and raised here,
And my dad and granddad before me.
I stick to the old ways.
I ain't seen no reason yet
To give up independence for convenience.
I light my own candle
And I don't owe a dime.
My son and grandson are the same way.
Give 'em a clearing in the woods
And they can start a fire,
Raise a cabin,
Make a table and put food on it.
Just feel this homespun.
You can't buy stuff like this
The way my wife makes it,
Warm as toast, and waterproof, too.
She can make any camp cosy
And brew up a cup o' tea
That'll cure what ails you.
We got no call to be ashamed.
We can look any man right in the eye
And say we never lied nor cheated
To make a living.
There's virtue in survival.
You modern folks with your new-fangled ideas
May disapprove of how we see things,
But I tell you here and now
That it's okay to be alive
And make a path through the grass.

Wild Sunflower (*Helianthus annuus*)

No nerves, nor eyes,
And yet I gaze face to face
Upon that ultimate sunflower
And wonder what huge amazing pollinators it calls,
Although it never seems to fill and droop
As I do now
Above Earth's cupped hands;
She has promised
That what seeds escape the beaks
She will plant.

The Seasons (Douglas Fir)

How pure is the line of snow on the branch.
How delicate are the tracks left when the kinglet flies.

In spring the presents are finally opened.
When the tissue paper is torn off—ah! enough perfume for
 another year!

Now the sun gets out a fine brush and some white paint
And carefully highlights each needle.

How delicate is the line left by the spider.
How pure are the beaded raindrops.

The Gambler (Collecting Seed From Chocolate Lily, *Fritillaria lanceolata*)

You act surprised to find me sporting pants
And spending chips from stacks of tidy piles,
A pack of cards like autumn in my hands;
My cronies fan their cards to hide their smiles.
It's been a while since you were here last spring.
I wore my fancy silk, as I recall;
I'm not beguiling in my oldest things,
But I'm no less myself, enhanced by fall.
You say I'm foolish, yet you want to know
Why I let chancy bets use up my stores:
I know the things I hoard will never grow;
I let them go in order to have more.
    Here—take these chips—and change out of your frown
    And take a chance on life, and cast them down.

Ornamental

If only Christmas came in fall,
I'd never decorate at all.
I'd hide my gifts in piles of leaves
Outside beneath the apple trees.

Talking Charades #1

I am small and gentle.
Sometimes you worship me,
Sometimes you use me,
Sometimes you spurn me.
But when you smell me, you love me.
I am my mother's blanket.
I am the ultimate metaphor.

What am I?

Talking Charades # 2

I am an artist.
I love to work wet-on-wet in oils.
I paint in my pajamas,
And I never eat breakfast
Until I have filled a canvas.
Then I give it to the first person who says, "Oh, how beautiful!"
I never copyright my work.
In fact, I dare you to copy it.

What am I?

Talking Charades #3

Call me Puck.
I love to steal kisses.
I love women in big hats and fluffy dresses.
I love still water, clean sheets, uncut fields.
I play the same joke over and over again.
If the joke is right,
It never stops being funny.

What am I?

Talking Charades #4

These are the things I love:
Bare feet,
Earthworms,
Eager fingers,
Toy shovels,
Baby grass,
Paws and claws,
Boot treads,
Fallen petals.
This is my motto:
I stick with the things I love.

What am I?

Talking Charades #5

Some of you grownups hate me
And keep trying to kill me,
But I don't care
Because children everywhere love me
And I love them.
For them I will turn into toy after toy.
I'm the sunlight in your homemade Walden.
I'm the goldfinch laughter of your lawn.

What am I?

Talking Charades #6

The smell of hard work
And of human feelings
Is strong,
But it is honorable
To work in my own support,
And I clean up pretty good.
Babies love my shelter,
And I am part of the hug you crave.

What am I?

Talking Charades #7

I am a pair of cupped hands.
I am a toy earth.
I am no good unless I am full of holes,
And I make a really dreadful hat.

What am I?

True Stories About The Hills

Oh, the bare fat hills
And the bony rocks!

Not far from here's a place a hermit lived,
Way up a hill among the towering rocks.
One morning he hiked up, and there he stayed,
And rested in the shadow of the cliff,
And wandered through the ripened spikes of grass,
The rusty seed heads and the dusty stones,
The glowing sunflowers and the pungent weeds,
And looked for buckwheat blooming softly pink.
He watched the sunset slowly stain the sky,
And made his mind up, as he watched it fade,
To sleep there, where he felt so much at ease.
(I bet he brought some water and a lunch,
And was no stranger to the earth's hard breast.)
When morning came he knew that he would stay.
He made a cave into a little house,
And for a garden, he let nature choose.
(He must have bought his food down in the town
And packed his fuel and water up the hill,
And what about an outhouse? Where was that?)
He told his visitors he liked the peace
And liked to watch the bustle down below.
The folks were close enough, but not too close.
We love the tall thin rock that marks the spot.
(Two stovepipes kept it company back then.)
We crane our necks whenever we drive by
To look up at that rock and think of him.
I'm glad the spot he chose was really steep,
Or else it might have been developed now

Like so much of the land around has been.
And that old graveyard spread out down below
Is much more overcrowded now as well.

Oh, the corrugated cliffs
And the sunny flowers with claws like hawks!

This place, unchanged for many years, still marred
By holes awash with pale collapsing space,
And overlooked by surly poison oak,
Is where pot-hunters came to spend their sweat.
Oh, Shakespeare is aghast to see them dig.
Not that again! You know, these holes are deep.
So now I know how holes in roads were named.
Now native plants have come to grow and bloom
Down all the sides and bottoms of the holes.
These flowers are the heroes of the scene.
These little bitty plants have great big hearts.
Somehow they have forgiven all those ones
Who dug where no one ever should have dug.
And yet, despite the kindness of the plants,
I have a funny feeling about these holes.

Look, the tiny outline of a deer
Beneath that sky-drawn tree.

Back then the hills were crowded full of sheep,
Those loud-mouthed busy nibblers with big hair.
They wrote their stories in cuneiform
Across the steepest faces of the hills.
They stamped their stylus hooves in stony dirt,
The very ground their tablets, time their now,
Inscribing lines and lines of hieroglyphs
(cont'd)

About the urgent search for further grass.
It almost seems the shepherds left no mark,
But some of their great-grandkids live nearby,
Now busy making stories of their own.

Look, there's the curve of a shoulder,
And trees for a mane.

They found a hidden place above the creek
Within the shelter of a horseback hill,
Protected from the wind and far from crowds,
Where hills at dawn and sunset, left and right,
Held colors that could make a painter cry.
They built a house here on this little knoll,
Perhaps it was a hundred years ago.
These fitted rocks remain, still neatly squared
To level up the ground beneath the walls.
What else? Some pieces of a broken crock,
Part of a stove, a handful of square nails,
A rusted dipper, bits of melted glass,
Is almost all the wildfires could well spare.
A harness buckle, rusted shut, once rode
A horse's back on day-long trips to town.
(And now it's just some minutes in a car.)
And here, an old forge tool, been lost for years,
With which he rang his anvil, backwoods bell;
Up at the house she heard him at his work,
And knew that all was well, and kept the beat
With feet strong on the treadle while she sewed.
The wheel that joined the treadle to the belt
Was foundered in the dirt, like his forge tool,
Unseen beneath the ground until this now.
As for the rest, did they cut trees, clear fields,
And plant a garden in this stony clay?
And maybe kept some chickens, milked a cow?

The pines here now are young enough to be
What sprouted when that him and her were gone.
Well, some things can be known, the rest is guess.
They say there was a settler's grave nearby.
I wish I knew just where to lay these flowers.

Mt. Hood stands on tiptoe to peer over the hills,
Sharp as flaked obsidian.

Two boys were hiking up a flat-topped hill
With lunches in their packs and happy mouths,
And as they wandered on the highest slopes,
They came across a silent hoop of rocks
The size of little pillows, more or less,
Still in the circle left when long ago
Some people pulled a tipi cover out
From under them, and packed, and went away.
The boys stood in the middle of the ring
And looked down at where once the others slept,
Then looked out at the view the others saw,
And wondered why they chose this very spot,
Not knowing it was once less desolate.
"Oh, hey, I bet we'll find an arrowhead!"
They searched, but no, not even a scorched rock,
No sign of why the others made their camp
On such a barren place up near the sky,
And they were gone too far away to ask.
So that was all the boys could tell their folks,
And late that night they lay in bed and thought:
So many stories lost out in the hills.

Oh, the bare fat hills
And the bony rocks!

On Our Anniversary

I never asked for diamonds, nor did you;
We felt that things intangible were more,
So much more worth the trouble of pursuit
Than all the spendy things that people hoard.
And yet despite all this—and it's held true
Through many years together on the trail—
You give me diamonds in their multitudes:
Not rocks—despite their twinkle dead as nails—
But living diamonds, warm and lovely things,
As generous and vital as the rain,
And just as full of rainbows. There's no ring
Or necklace I could value like these plain
    And pleasing drops of sweat that come to grace
    Your brow and luminate your much-loved face.

For My Husband On His Birthday

I love to think of lovely rounded things:
The gibbous moon that moons behind the pines;
A nest of eggs a robin nestles in;
A boulder, lichen-kissed, that lizards like;
A russet apple in the rustling leaves;
The rippling rings where rising fish have passed;
A warm-hued peach with rosy human cheeks;
The grassy hill where sunlight lingers last.
And you partake of nature's art as well:
You're one with all the lovely rounded ones;
I know there's times you wish your hair was full
And thick and young, but beauty also comes
    Where sun and moon and wind and rain have kissed
    (As I have kissed) your lovely roundedness.

The Hose End

Soon as I drop the hose to pull some weeds,
An eager little person comes to it;
With shining eyes she gets down on her knees
And tells me not to move that hose one bit;
And clear and sweet the water softly flows,
And clear and sweet she talks and sometimes sings;
Her hands, now plastered brown, now washed to rose,
Intent upon the work of making things;
And mountains rise, lakes deepen, rivers flood,
And reservoirs are built and filled and breached;
She shows me funny sounds she makes with mud,
And how a castle melts into a beach—
    My clutch of weeds is gone—our knees are wet—
    We're gonna make the biggest magic yet.

The Purple Iris

Back there the grass is short where grownups walk,
But here it tops a little person's head,
And when he goes around a big wild rock,
He finds a place that beckons him ahead:
Beyond he sees a vision, tall and true,
Both hidden and flamboyant in its wings,
All colored bright as if God's crayons were new—
He never dreamed that Earth could hold such things—
He starts out toward it, struggling through the grass,
And struggling over stones and through the weeds,
Now closer, closer, closer, till at last
He's made it, face to face with what he seeks—
    And now he reaches out to touch its face,
    And his is full of wonder and of grace.

The Perfect House

The house of my dreams
Is strong and broad and white
And spacious with windows and skylights
And wrapped around with a porch on all sides
Wide enough for a toddler to ride a trike
Past grownups in cushioned chairs, talking and laughing.
This house has big rooms
And big windows that open like doors.
Insects never come in, except butterflies and hover flies,
And also hummingbirds come in to explore,
And if you hold still,
They will all find their own way safely out again.
The sweet smell of flowers comes in,
And a green smell from the lawn that was cut early this morning,
And the cool air from under a shady tree
With strong low branches that invite children up.
This house of my dreams
Somehow always has clean floors
For little bare feet to patter on,
And fluffy clean carpets for babies to crawl on.
The laundry warm from the dryer is heaped in a basket,
The tables are always uncluttered,
The houseplants are exuberant,
The bookcases are too full,
The chairs are covered with soft blankets,
And the couch is long enough
For a tired person to stretch out
With feet up on a pillow.
Everything is washable one way or another,
And nobody gets upset if you accidentally spill something.
And everywhere there are flowers,

Huge extravagant bouquets in magically unbreakable vases,
That sometimes at special moments a hummingbird will visit.
A savory smell is drifting from the kitchen,
And a finch sings near the feeder in the yard.
In this house of my dreams,
Children get out paper and crayons,
And shake rattles and tambourines,
And push little cars across the floor,
And the people in this house feel like painting something,
Or writing a poem,
Or learning another musical instrument,
Or helping a child up onto their lap
And telling a story they make up as they go along.
On the walls are taped up the children's drawings,
And photographs of friends,
And behind them are tucked leaves and feathers found on walks.
When you come to visit,
Be sure to take the toys and books out of the chair
Before you sit down,
Feel free to put your feet up,
And remember not to say any unkind word
In this house of my dreams.

How Shall I Describe The New Moon?

I feel sorry for her empty arms,
But at least I know
That she will soon be pregnant.

The tide has gone out,
Leaving this little shell fragment
Inlaid in the sand.

It looks like
God has been
Cutting his fingernails again!

Surely there is an old legend
That tells how White Buffalo Woman
Got up in the sky.

The pine tree is growing out her bangs.
Now they are long enough
To need a clip.

A broken shell in the middle of the grass
Means that the mother bird has cleaned her nest.
Is there ever an albino raven?

It would take a really big medicine woman
And more love than I have
To mend this broken hoop.

Yet when she dances with a planet,
Somehow I feel excited again
About finding the path of beauty.

How Shall I Describe The Full Moon?

At first I thought it was a dream,
But no matter how long I watched,
The bubble did not pop.

Excuse me!
I have to rush inside
And heap my bowl with vanilla ice cream!

God was very tired when he emptied his pockets,
And he did not pick up this one dime
That fell and rolled away across the floor.

Long ago, some very cold people
Were puzzling over how to build a house out of snow
Until the moon said, "Look at me!"

I don't see a man up there.
I see a little child just finishing a chocolate treat
While the mommy runs for a wet washcloth.

Now this is enough
To make any little hen worth its salt broody.
How long till it hatches?

These orange streetlights are an insult to her beauty,
But she keeps on rising.
She is above such things.

Go ahead, count all the hawks.
But if you're going to stare at her all night,
Remember to tell her that you love her.

City Crow

Within his black cloak
lurk rainbows of color
That gleam and shift as he bends
to peck apart the intricacies
of a dead lunch, dashed
down by feckless hands—
look out!—here comes a dog.
Burnished wings unfurl,
grant to ears that wild sound:
feathers gripping the air;
black claws click on top of a sign (NO LOITERING).
The human hurries, heedless,
pulls the scavenger nose away
toward that ordained place and time
always just ahead.

A shining eye observes
an ally glide and swoop,
alight, approach,
invert the prize with glossy beak,
pin it with dexterous feet, extricate a vital morsel.
The observer lifts his sable epaulets,
brandishes his beak,

bells out an exuberant message.
He takes to the dingy air,
slides a glissando over downbent heads,
trailing a fulgent cloak—
sparks of light and wind.

Why does he remain
in these perilous canyons?
Above the persistent scruff of weeds
at the foot of the sign (NO LOITERING),
he sings on,
an undeciphered voice.

Waiting For Paradise By A
No-Trespassing Sign

Listen.
We are the dispossessed,
the ones without gardens.
We are priced out,
kicked out,
zoned out,
fenced out.
We are told to move out.
Really, there is not much space left to be out in.

We are too poor
to buy justice.
We are thirsty
for the milk of human kindness,
but it does not seem to flow
past the bottom line.
The world is full of strangers
who are each other's friend
but not ours.

It is tough to keep forgiving people
who do not even know they need it.
Being right gives them hard faces.
Yet what a burden not to forgive!

We are tired of hearing
that anyone can have a garden.
That coffee can full of dirt
just doesn't cut it.
We are children of Adam, too.

Well, it looks like they're starting another development.
We can't help wondering:
will the meek still want the earth
when the proud are done with it?

The Acorn (*Quercus garryana*)

No, Hamlet has not been here. If he had,
He would have seen how very big a dream's
Encompassed by my shell: a noble plan,
Complete in every part from germ to seam,
Distilled, condensed, intensified, compact,
Thus rounded to a lovely oval fit
That's neither loose nor tight; no room, in fact,
For any second thoughts or thoughtless fits:
Forget the zero—empty brittle clown;
Forget infinity—it is a cheat.
And yet there's room here, Hamlet, room to count
The still-uncounted wonders of the seed,

    A living dream that grows, not for a king,
    But simply for the song it has to sing.

The Encampment (Paper Birch In Spring)

The tribe has pitched their tipis here
Where grass is thick and water near,
And high above, the red-tails veer and circle down to mate.

The lodgepoles angle up so high,
They hug the ground, they kiss the sky,
And from their tips the streamers fly like birds across a field.

The tipi covers, neatly made
And winter-weathered, glow and fade
As sunrise light and sunset shade give shape to every trait.

In sudden wind the lodgepoles hum—
Right here both past and vision come
To welcome travellers to the drum till every one is healed.

When Deer Brush Deer Brush
(*Ceanothus integerrimus*)

In the saturated green of evening
When the sun is behind the hill,
The doe swims among the blossoms,
Her warm brown coat awash
In soft blue and white, like foamy hands,
And as she floats forward
To take a colored bite,
Guard hairs brush petals,
Silk on silk,
Touch, and slide, and separate,
Gently pressed together by their respective bodies,
A moment interleaved like tesselated fingers,
Then springing to their usual arc,
Each with a lingering memory of the other.
Now the doe's back is flecked with tiny flowers,
Blue, and white, and almost purple,
And on the tresses of bloom, a few brown hairs.
How rich the gentle colors in the evening.

The Shaman (Fairy Slipper, *Calypso bulbosa*)

I have come back from a long journey to be with you.

Yes, the petroglyphs are true,
As you can see from my aura.

Here, let me open my pouch
And show you these simple things
That have become treasures.

Perhaps you only see dirt around me,
But I assure you my spirit helper is here.
Take my hand and I will help you
With your own journey.

The Acting Troupe (Mariposa Lily, *Calochortus macrocarpus*)

This little glade will be our stage;
These trees and rocks our scenery make;
This shady log will be the place where critics get enchanted.

A comedy is what we'll raise,
With hose in hose and plays in plays,
A spell of Shakespeare that you may remember ever after.

Our costumes are of stuff so fine,
With subtle tints and lovely lines,
Embroidered in a rare design, embossed, and plumed, and banded.

Consider as you watch our play:
Our every move holds yours at bay;
Our speeches hold you in speechless sway except for tears
                    and laughter.

Composite Family

A little flower called to me.
I knelt down in the dirt to see.
It lifted up a yellow face
That held a slender little bee.

I leaned too quickly in my haste—
The bee was gone without a trace.
I grabbed a leaf and shook its hand,
A green and soft and downy grace.

I had to know its name. I fanned
The pages of my guidebook, scanned
A fashion show of rayon blends,
A family album of a clan.

The bee came humming back just then;
The flower breathed a gentle scent;
I could not name it in the end,
So we just called each other "Friend."

In The Forest Of Possibilities

I came to crossroads in the woods
And stopped to think my choices out,
And each road lay in sun and shade
Like lazy dogs and rainbow trout;
I looked and hummed and scratched and stood
But could not tell which way was best;
The crossroads made a charming glade,
So I sat down to think and rest.
To give up, as I thought, for good
One road to choose the other one
Was what I meant to contemplate,
But stopped before I had begun.
A bird streaked paint across the woods;
A gleaming beetle mapped a leaf;
A spider strung a harp and played
A song that insects might believe;
Then something zig-zagged through the woods
And came and hovered, eye to eye,
And landed, and aligned its blades:
A freshly painted dragonfly,
So close to me that I could look
At all the etching on its wings,
Its hand-carved back with stars inlaid—
Who needs a muse who has this thing?
It sprang, as light as if it took
More work to tether to a twig;
I jumped up, too, with lesser grace,
And tried to chase each zag and zig—
To get yet closer if I could—

By turns it vanished, then it flashed—
By turns I had to stop and wait,
Then hurry after as it passed—
And then it zoomed up, gone for good,
And left me like a dreamer there.
Behind me was the little glade;
Ahead a road curved on somewhere.
I figured out just where I stood:
I'd come far up the right-hand way,
So I went on through sun and shade;
I said, "This road will be okay."

An Idea Of Beauty

I love roses.
What do roses love?
Manure heaped up
and water splashed on.

I love butterflies.
What do butterflies love?
Manure spread around
to soak in the puddles.

When I come
pushing another wheelbarrow load,
all tired out and sweaty,
smelling like a barnyard
and far from clean,
it's nice to know
that lovely creatures
love what's made
this mess of me.

The Dancer (Oriental Poppy)

At last she flings off her robes,
Unfolds a fascination of pink,
Belling open as she spins,
Exposing hidden panels
Richly stained with a
Gorgeous saturated inky tone that
Is composed of all the colors,
Not their absence; revealing in this so-short dance
Everything she has dreamed of for so long.

Field Trip To The Habitat Restoration Project In The Old Quarry, Or, Columbia Desert Parsley (*Lomatium columbianum*)

We come to where the earth is deeply hurt
And thinly spread with living medicine,
And there we wander with our searchlight eyes
To see if any seeds have woken up
And stretched their arms above their rocky beds.
We travel slow and clumsy on the rocks
That shift and grate beneath our shifting feet;
We call and point and gather round each sprout—
Our feet must seem like giant feet to them—
And here a transplant has relaxed its fists
And promised to outgrow its little crib.
We slowly wend our way across a scene
That seems to be just barren empty gray
With here and there a sleepy grayish stick,
Until we blink our visionary eyes
And seem to see what it may someday be
When all the sticks and seeds are fully grown
And married, and have children of their own.

At length we pause beneath a rocky cliff
To rest our eyes and feet on something green.
We bend above a topsy-turvy plant
That's fallen from the cliff's eroding crown
And wonder what it was, now half-decayed.
We feel like we've been looking down for hours;
We straighten up and stretch and gaze around

And call each other eagerly to come
And see the first wild flower of the year.
There, halfway up the cliff, it calmly sits
As if on folded blankets, and its robes
Are buckskin thickly sewn with purple beads.
Some force has brought us here together now
At just this single lovely spot in time.
We lift our heads and see it sitting there
And pointing up, and so we all look up,
And just as we look up, way up the cliff
To where the rocks intrude upon the sky—
The blue blue sky, with clouds so paper-white,
As swift and ragged as a child can rip—
A bald eagle soars out overhead
And circles over us, and comes again.
"A bald eagle! Look!" we call out loud,
And then fall silent, wide-eyed to the sky,
And we begin to feel that nothing else
Has ever been so dark brown and so white
As this one perfect bird above us now.
It gazes down with telescopic eyes
And sees us with our eager upstretched arms;
It sees the medicine spread on this place
Where Earth is hurt, and cannot heal herself,
And seems to bless us with its beating wings.
We watch until it circles out of sight,
Then slowly go our various separate ways,
But in our thoughts we're still beneath those wings
And tell ourselves that someday roots will win
And rocks will not shift underfoot again.

Autumn Orchestra

The year's great day revolves toward afternoon.
Seeds rattle in their pods.
Spiders pluck their webs,
strong in their annual kingdom.
Call notes ring from reddening orbs:
crab apples, rose hips, honeysuckle berries.
Beak people flute from twig to twig.
Hide-and-seek insects shrill out a descant.
Player after player greatens the symphony
Until finally—
Fortissimo!

Don't Believe Everything You Read

Some gardener writes that nature is no gardener.
If Nature is no gardener, what are we?
Where man has not defiled it, there's more art in her
Little finger...think of tropic trees
Ornate with orchids, think of grassy locks
Alive with flower eyes, of fern-draped cliffs
Where clear drops fall, of ruminating rocks
Surrounding sun-raked sand...and count the gifts
She gives to all her creatures: living space,
And plants for food, and water's lively touch,
And air and light for every upturned face,
And dirt for gardens. Let who does as much
   Come throw that first hard stone. But please don't leave:
   She wants to hire some gardeners who believe.

Hidden

There is a pain too shy for any words,
That shrinks from any touch like the horns of a snail,
That lives under the dead leaves and fallen branches,
And when disturbed, prefers to close its door.
It says, please believe in the camouflage of my shell.

There is a grief that renounces words,
Like a mysterious bulb
That every year is deeper in the earth,
Unsuspected by the sunlight creatures.
Some years there is enough rain for a flower
That withers, bittersweet.

There is a hurt so bright it hides its face
And will not look, no matter what the time,
Like that day in November
That seems to be all evening.

Oh, well. Surely something needs repotting.
There are some small but potent joys:
The smell and the feel of newly sifted compost,
Lifted, sniffed, and mixed by hand
With perlite and a dash of kelp;
The satisfaction of getting the little plant
In the very center of its new pot.

The Trumpet Player (California Poppy)

Come try our lofty concert hall,
As long and wide as it is tall;
Come sit on stage between us all and soak the music in.

Our bright conductor nears his stand;
He mounts his box and lifts his hand;
I raise my horn at his command beneath this tall blue ceiling.

With breath so strong and yet so light,
I bring forth notes so clear and bright
They soar and float and play and kite like eagles on the wind.

My high notes travel like a bee
From heart to heart so pure and free;
They touch a Haydn's ear and he writes music till he's dreaming.

Lines To Write In A Homemade Valentine

You are my metaphor.
Your eyes are lighted candles.
Your nose is a playground slide.
Your ears are secret caves in the rimrock.
Your mouth is a pot of spaghetti.
Your hair is a stream pouring over a boulder.
Your feet are puppies.
Your hands are kittens.
Your stomach is a chocolate truffle.
Your belly button is the center of the universe.
Your hug is warm blankets.
Your smile is toast popping up out of the toaster.

I will look at you like Rembrandt looks.
I will hold you like a cup of hot cocoa.
I will hug you like they hug trees.

A Day In The Life Of The Porch

Above the steps,
The little tree stretches out its hands
To catch the sun.

See? This exact spot on the railing
Has been blessed
By a wren's claws.

I have carried away
All the pots with dead seedlings.
Now the porch is cheerful again.

The hummingbird hides behind the feeder.
One eye and a red cheek.
Yes, I am still holding still!

Now a watercolor cloud
Sweeps a brush loaded with gray,
Then breathes to dry its work.

Geraniums make the best pets.
They are so soft and gentle.
And they have flowering paws.

This old garage-sale bench
Is better
Than any throne.

Book Two

What The Sun Said

I think that Earth is such a lovely thing,
So rich with color as it slowly turns,
Intensely blue, so many greens in spring,
And browns of every hue from gold to burnt,
And, oh! the zebras! and the blooming trees!—
You say what? From Larch Mountain you looked down
And saw things as you think I always see?
What other way is there to look but down?
What do you mean, you like to see me rise?
And how could all the leaves just glow in spring?
You say that overhead you've got blue skies?
You have a shadow? What's this rainbow thing?
   Perhaps it's really true (though who knows why?)
   There's more to people than what meets the eye.

At Play

A stone lies on its chest among the herbs,
As smooth and square as part of an old beam,
A fossil of a barn, a noun whose verbs
Are tulips growing close; and highlights gleam
On rich dark-purple petals, almost black;
One drowsy flower head, yet to expand,
Is hanging down above the stone's warm back,
A blown and painted egg in a dancer's hand—
A cat in striped pajamas comes to play;
Bright-eyed, it lifts a small blackberry paw
And taps that tulip's cheek and makes it sway,
And taps it back twice more, with never a claw,
    A kid with a balloon—then tilts an ear
    And skips hence, leaving someone laughing here.

Early

This tulip, soft and pink as someone's cheek,
That rides its rocking stem in the gentle air,
Is open just enough to give a peek
Inside a living room, and hidden there
A little person safely, soundly sleeps,
Dressed in the finest velvet, inky black
Just touched with lemon yellow, and she keeps
Her eyes wide open as she dreams on back
To morning, sunny morning, full of flowers,
And somewhere there's a nest site just for her.
Not long now, and she'll shiver up her powers
And buzz up through the skylight, strong and sure—
    This tulip, when Sun buzzes from its doze
    Will open wide enough for someone's nose.

Barn Yarns

Ponies nickery,
Chickens bickery.

Cats sinuous,
Roosters dinuous.

Pigs muddly,
Cows cuddly.

Tractors parkable,
Dogs barkable.

The Bibliophile (Pearly Everlasting, *Anaphalis margaritacea*)

So here's my special hoard of books.
I savor them like twenty cooks.
It's neat to read the words that hook some slippery truth at last.

The pages in their density,
Aligned and sewn so carefully,
Invite a thumb to come release the rustle that's within.

I've read them often, I confess,
But I'm not full, and they're not less;
I pick the ones I like the best, like flowers from the past.

It's not their rareness, nor their dates,
Nor yet their cost that fascinates:
It's just that they've become my mates through times both
        thick and thin.

In Fall

God is walking on the hills in the wind.
He walks through the trees with his face uplifted
And his long white hair streaming back.
Yellow leaves fly on the wind,
And he stoops to pick one up.
He touches its cold smooth surface to his cheek,
And runs his finger gently along the little teeth on its edge,
Then releases it to fly to a new resting place,
While the wind flaps God's white robes
And races past, pulling a toy cloud on a string.
A red-tailed hawk calls,
And God tilts his head to watch it circle.
He spreads his arms wide to catch the wind in his robes
And runs down a little slope.
"What a glorious day," he says. "Come play with me!"

Sizes

If I were really really big,
I would stroke the firm plush flanks of the hills,
I would brush the springy fir-textured forest,
I would test the half-sharpened points of the mountains,
I would breathe the wind.

If I were really really small,
I would curl up inside a little cup-shaped flower
And live on its fair breath
And lick up bright liquid nectar,
And at night, the silken petals would gently close around me.

If I were just my size
And had hands like mine,
I would touch a feather,
And the moss growing up a tree trunk.
I would walk in the ocean of air.
And I would let a kitten touch me
With those cushiony pads on the bottoms of its paws
And with its rough little tongue.

Marble-ous

The rain cloud came and shook its marble bag
And challenged the whole garden to a game;
The broccoli alone took up the brag,
Stood up and calmly made a counterclaim;
At once the cloud hurled down the worst it had—
It sent its marbles pelting thick and fast—
But nothing fazed the broccoli a tad,
Though all the carrots flattened in the blast...
By noon the growling cloud had trailed away,
A-grump and dragging its now-empty tote;
And left behind in each blue leaf there lay
A hard-won marble, round as any note,
   A living crystal gem that, now it's manned,
   Rolls magically in each leafy hand.

Weedacious

Beyond the edge where no one digs or hoes,
There grows a patch of scruffy tangled weeds
Where redroot bristles, feral carrot blows,
And prickly lettuce spangles fluffy seeds;
A pointy insect guards a mottled leaf,
And spiders drape their tatting everywhere;
A feline thistle shows its claws and teeth,
And mullein masquerades as something rare.
This place is just a white space on the map
Beyond the fat well-tended garden beds,
And no one ever tries to make a path
Through all these knotted vines and scratchy heads;
   But it's a place where butterflies are seen,
   And mornings, it wears diamonds like a queen.

Peas

Peas are vegetable babies.
They squeak
And they cling so tightly to their trellis
With their curly little tendrils.
Their leaves are so smooth,
Their blooms are so soft.
And see how fast they grow!
Their pods are toys clutched and brandished.
They hold them out,
But you still have to get them out of their fists.
Each pod splits with a wonderful little pop,
And inside the toy peas are lined up,
So neat and round and orderly,
Ready to be nibbled right out of the pod.
Each pea detaches with a satisfying little snap,
And crunches with a delicate little crunch,
Full of sweet green juice.
Are there ever enough pea pods?
Each one is a secret green world,
A row of tiny people in a canoe,
Little dolls lined up in a doll bed,
A family in a small cosy house.
It's okay to eat them up.
And it's okay to drop the pod halves on the ground.
They will go back to Mother Earth.
Look—a little bitty pod is pushing out of this blossom!
It must be a dolly pod!
And here are some that will be ready tomorrow!
Oh, peas are worth it!

Inside A Crookneck Squash

The knife cuts a straight clean paisley slice,
Shining with life,
The rind cool and yellow as pressed butter,
The layer inside a warm, yielding white,
Cells glistening;
Inside that, the future seeds in cross-section, so thick
You could cross the river on their backs,
Their hearts tinted green,
Their shells still soft as molted crawdads,
Their tender cotyledons sweet with juice;
And between them all, across the middle,
A map of the old pollen highway.
When the slice is bent,
The seeds open and close like the mouths of antiphonal singers;
When the slice breaks,
The seeds heave like whale-backs out of the foam,
The mother-water parting around them.
The rind is firmly crunchy,
The outer rim of flesh soft,
The inner sea of flesh almost too soft,
The seeds slippery and delicately crunchy,
The flavor mild as spring air...
And now the slice is gone,
Savored, devoured,
Finished, vanished;
And already its predator is plotting
Just where the crooknecks should go
Next year.

How To Make A Good Breakfast

First comes the sacred dirt.
If only everyone had the dirt they need!
If you got dirt, give thanks.

Next comes the seed, also sacred.
Heads almost clunk over the pictures in the catalogs.
What names!
Painted Mountain, Black Aztec,
Mandan Bride, Nothstine Dent,
Seneca Red Stalker, Longfellow Flint...
How to choose?

Then comes the sweat.
Planting seems like it should be easy,
But actually it's the hardest part.
Dig, dig, dig,
Rake, rake, rake,
Hoe, hoe, hoe.
Stoop a hundred times,
Or kneel, getting your knees caked with mud,
Or crawl along the rows.
When you see an old-fashioned corn planter,
You know those old-timers were smart.
Children lose interest long before it's done.
Well, supper's gonna be simple tonight, that's for sure.

Leaves in view! O! The joy!

Now the corn is tall enough to hide in.
As you go past dragging a hose,
Pretend you don't hear those little giggles

And let the children jump out and surprise you.
Then crawl in after them,
Into a secret green jungle.
Sure, there's compaction.
But hey, the plants can use the extra carbon dioxide.

In case of a windstorm,
A web of clothesline tied to a pitchfork
Firmly pushed into the dirt
Will save the lives of these tall brothers and sisters.

Then the rustles change from green to pale tan.
Now comes the very best part:
It's the sound children make
When they snap off a first ear
And peel back the wrapping in a strip
And expose a row of shining many-colored teeth:
"OOOOOOOOooooooooooooo!"

Returning with a wheelbarrow
Loaded, filled, heaped with ears,
While the children dance alongside,
Is a moment for trumpets.

Time to unwrap the presents!
The husks squeak as they are pulled back,
And the naked ears roll noisily around on the kitchen table.
And of course the silk must be made into wigs.
What a mess!
And the colors!
Wow, corn kernels can be pink,
Or lavender, or aqua, or jade,

(cont'd)

Or lemon striped with orange,
Or midnight blue, or saturated red,
Or gamboge, or deepest aubergine.
Running our hands along the rows,
Our fingertips hear music,
Perhaps harpsichord and an oboe.

Sitting in a cornstalk tipi,
You can feel the conical wisdom, snug around you,
Just like they felt it long ago,
Ancestors upon ancestors.

Then the ears dry.
The kernels shrink and lose their shine.
And here's something children like to do:
Rub two ears together and pop the kernels off.
What a racket!
No matter how big your dishpan,
Kernels will escape in all directions.
Days later, they are still getting found
Behind the cookbooks or under the toaster.
You might recall that legend
About the person whom Corn and Bean blessed
Because he kept stopping in the trail
To pick up every little seed
That fell out of people's baskets.

It might be nice to keep the empty cobs handy
In case you suddenly have to groom a horse,
Or smoke some meat,
Or build a toy cabin.

Now to grind them into meal.
Some people buy mills,
Or you can use your blender.
Down by the Big River
There are some holes in the rocks
Where the Old Ones came to pound their stuff,
Holes that are centuries deep.

Now, finally, the cooking.
It's very simple in the end:
Three cups water and one cup cornmeal;
Simmer gently with some honey and a bit of salt.
All winter, this meal will make sunshine inside you.
Welcome to the circle of life!

Now...
    ...if only everyone could have dirt.

Talking Charades #8

I am lightning in your hands.
A flash arcs down,
Strikes with a splitting crack,
And thunder rumble-tumbles out to each side.
If you love me, I get extremely intelligent.
And did you know,
My great-great-granddaddy was a bird of prey?

What am I?

Talking Charades #9

Me and my wife are builders.
We build our own home,
Wearing old canvas coats and flannel shirts.
Gotta choose wood that's just right,
Well-seasoned and strong.
We haul it ourselves.
We work at our own pace
And it all gets done at the right time.
Beauty and usefulness together
Make perfect symmetry.
You know, plaster's better than panelling,
And we like those old-fashioned straw ticks.
When everything's ready,
My wife moves in her pottery—
The most beautiful porcelain,
Hand-painted, lightly glazed,
Inspired by the sky,
A joy to look at—
But we never invite anyone over.
We prefer to live secluded.
Privacy is how we feel okay,
And that's that.

What am I?

Talking Charades #10

I am small,
But I am essential for the joy of many creatures.
I range high in the sky
And I burrow down in the earth.
Sometimes I sing
And sometimes I am silent.
I am really strong and clever
And I am really weak and fragile.
And I was essential to Shakespeare.

What am I?

Talking Charades #11

I am so smooth, I seem to be soft,
Even though I'm not.
Despite my rough-and-tumble past,
I am eager to be friends.
It only takes me a few minutes
To warm up to you.
The only thing I fear is an ostrich.

What am I?

Talking Charades #12

I am snow not yet walked on.
I am moonlight on the floor.

I hate sunbathing.
I can die in a moment,
But I may well outlast you.
I love toddlers, children, writers, artists.
Their touch is immortality.

What am I?

Talking Charades #13

Long ago, I had wings and flew on the wind.
After that, I had lots of arms.
Now I have only a neck and a body.

Contrary to the rumors,
I have never hurt a cat.

How I love to be close to you.
Hold me, massage me, love me,
And I will empower your soul.

What am I?

Talking Charades #14

I am a fish-eye lens,
And you are the camera.

I am my own magic trick:
I appear out of nowhere,
then vanish into thin air.

You really are as special
As you wish you were.
Here—have a halo that only you can see.

What am I?

Talking Charades #15

I am my own birthday present,
And I am the best present ever.
What's more, I open myself,
And then I quickly give myself
To the first person I see,
All the while singing my own birthday song.

What am I?

Talking Charades #16

In the Renaissance,
I was a monk.

In the Baroque period,
I was one of the nobility.

In the Romantic age,
I became an artist.

Now things are really modern.
My mind is a scientist.
My body is an animal.

What am I?

Paracatz

I am a hand trap
And a heart trap
Baited with a purr.

I am softer, smoother, sweeter
Than you.
I am sharper than you.

Food, food, give me food! Please!
Thanks! Yum! Delicious!
Okay, goodby for now! Who needs you?

Ah, birds!
I love 'em so much!
How come they never want to play?

I am a jungle hunter,
Master of the stalk...*invisible*...
Hey! How'd you know I was here?

Okay, hold still and I'll fix you up
With some good smells.
Oh, *ugh!* Why'd you have to touch me?

You're not obeying me!
But I love you anyway.
Shall we dance?

Doggerel

So here's a tale about a guy named Derwent Borden.
His wife had quite a passion for th' old-fashioned rose;
Their garden was a veritable paradise
(Save winter, when she pruned each branch back to a stalk);
But somehow Derwent had a feeling that there oughter
Be room in this fair Eden for a pair o' dogs.

Darlene said, "'Dogs in gardens' is a paradox!
My splendid borders would be turned into a boar den
By slobbery smelly beasts that poop just like an otter
Smack dab in all the paths, and dig up all the rows,
Galumph the grass to mud, and chase the neighbor's stock!"
She burst in tears, and showed old Der one pair red eyes.

"Why can't you get a bird?" she cried. "Let's parrotize!
A parrot's loyal, it learns tricks, a parrot talks—"
He crossed his arms and stood as stubborn as a stock.
He said, "I don't want some old bird. Why, I'd be bored in
No time flat!" She said, "How 'bout a nice dog rose?
It's got a bark, it scratches, and it smells! Aw, Der!"

The sun set as they argued back and forth with aught ter
Show for it. Der felt that it would parodize
His hankering for dogs to get a measly rose.
Darlene's eyes sparked in anger bright as peridots.
That night things didn't seem too rosy in the Borden
House, and scary parrot dreams were on the stalk.

Well, Der rose rueful with a ruse to raise his stock:
He'd get Dar some dog roses. Roses usually awed 'er.
Then she'd know his darling was still Darlene Borden.
He searched the nurseries to stock her paradise,
But bad luck dogged him like a pair o' dogs,
And all he found was one half-wilted doggy rose.

Der moped on home and gave Darlene that scraggly rose.
She said, "Surprise! Come meet King Arfer and Knight Stock!"
And there, with pink rosettes for collars, was a pair o' dogs!
Darlene was pleased as punch with how she'd awed Der.
Two dogs, as bright and playful as a pair o' dice,
Came wagging up to their new owner, Derwent Borden.

This little paradox—rose dogs and a dog rose—
Appeased a pair named Borden, who, when they took stock,
Thought there could be no odder, sweeter paradise.

Spiders I Have Known

One

A stem of summer grass was lightly streaked
With grassy green and palest yellow-tan,
And clinging like a lemur child was one
As slender, and as finely streaked with green,
Its legs aligned in longitudinal pairs;
And as it saw me moving to get close,
It sidled like a squirrel on a trunk
And vanished right behind that giant stem.

Two

A log lay on the earth, its bark long gone,
The weathered texture of its grain exposed,
The dark and darker stripes a perfect match
For those of a small hunter plateau'd there,
Whose one small move was all that caught my eye;
I thought, that lovely camouflage would look
Just positively horrid in a tub.

Three

I think I'll lightly pass over that time
When some appalling monster, way too big,
However clever it may be with web,
Repulsively malformed and witchy-legged,
And stained a pallid yellow, was released
During devotions, and had great success
In totally dismantling the sweet calm
Of that most popular and pretty girl
Who, unexpectedly, sat next to me.

Four

A row of giant sisters starred the deck
That ran outside a rustic laundromat,
Each at the hub of a substantial web
Well-cabled to the railing and the roof.
I found them scary, but upon the whole
No hindrance to me, trundling loads of clothes.
Too bad they caught a modern Avery's eye.
He popped the creatures out among the cars
And ripped their superstructures into rags
Despite the way his girlfriend grabbed his arm
And yelled at him to "Stop it! That's their home!"
I wonder if she ever figured out
What shadow drove him to ignore her words?
I wonder if she chose to stay with him,
Or if he'd broken more than webs that day.

Five

As I was sitting on a wooden bench,
I saw a prowling predator approach,
Wearing a tiger suit in black and white,
As brilliant as a keyboard packed with notes;
It searched with eyes like huge binoculars,
Then, poised beside a bottomless crevasse,
It swayed on jointed legs to judge the space,
Then jumped so fast it did not even blur.
One quick-split second, here, the next one, there.
The sun, that brash alchemist, flung a spell
That turned the white to shining silver stripes,
The black to richly burnished glistening gold;
Thus ornamented, topped with opal eyes,

(cont'd)

And trailing its prismatic bungee silk,
This fierce aggressor fearlessly advanced
On my foolhardy pencil's rubber end,
Reared up on its hind legs, and in a flash
It leaped up on this strange eraser thing—
Itself so small it barely spanned the end—
And then jumped off, and then attacked again,
Then, having found it neither friend nor foe,
Ignored its further blandishments and left.
I saw this hunter later going past,
A captured bug held crosswise in its mouth,
A tiger making off with that day's meat.

Six

A web was stretched between some tilted twigs
And caught the light like some old masterpiece;
A small brown artist held the center spot,
Each sensitive appendage spread just so,
And by some inspiration I reached down
And got a small fir needle from the path
And gently tossed it into that bright scene,
And instantly its owner came to life
And bustled angrily to get that mote
And extricate it with the greatest care,
Its claws as nimble as a set of hands.
It let the needle fall, disdainfully,
Then went back to the center of the world,
Though it did not repaint the ruined spot.

Seven

One day I got up early and went out
To see the sunrise tribe in dancing clothes.
Each grass blade held a tiny sphere of light.

My feet soaked up the light and left dark tracks,
And in the east the dance had just begun;
And there between two baby Douglas firs,
Still in the earth's gray shadow, was a web,
A perfect web, new-made, all strung with pearls,
Small elfin pearls formed of pellucid dew,
And hanging in the center, motionless,
The owner, covered in the same cold jewels,
A picture begging for a camera lens.
The sky tribe frolicked in their glowing clothes
As their big polished dance floor slowly turned
From rose to saffron to bright daffodil.
The sun peeked over Earth's rim with one eye,
And next to me the first light touched the web.
At once the small bespangled spider moved.
A front leg, slowly, slowly, stiff with cold,
Rose upward to the shoulder opposite
And slowly scraped its claw down that long leg,
Collecting all the droplets as it went;
All coalesced into one great big drop
That dangled there from that opposing leg,
And then the claw knocked it off into space.
One leg was free. The favor was returned,
And leg by leg the little creature worked;
Its back legs neatly scraped its body clean,
Discarding all the burden of its jewels.
It hung there gently basking in the sun,
The first arachnid ever I admired,
Though I suppose it didn't feel the same—
My camouflage was not the thing at all—
Just positively horrid next to web.

At The Dufur Threshing Bee

Two giant horses stand here quietly;
They make a couplet with a lovely rhyme,
Both golden as the stubble underhoof,
With manes and tails vanilla, while their man
As patiently explains to all the folks
Some things about his mares, who wear their gear
Like strong men wearing tank tops in the heat.
Their shapes are such a pleasure to the eye:
Their backs are hilltops tall against the hills;
Their sides are outlined in calligraphy;
Their haunches are French horns that play baroque;
Their legs are straight from Leonardo's dreams;
Their hooves are dictionaries (unabridged).
Ten daddies could hold up ten little girls
To brush and brush and brush and brush their manes.
Their man says, yes, sure, we can pet them some.
How warm and firm they are, how very big.
Up close they've got a strong warm horsey smell.
This one we're petting doesn't seem to mind.
My hand's a handkerchief impelled to fly
Straight to the big warm fuzzy sock of her nose,
Electric from the dryer, whisker-rayed,
A snowy scrap of flannel stuck to the toe.
Her nostrils flare, her breath puffs on my hand—
And suddenly she snorts—my hand jerks back—
A toddler, lifted up to pat her neck,
Is now convinced that there be dragons here—
And now's their turn to plow. Stand back a bit.
Their man, the gathered reins in his gloved hand,

Now clambers up to his small metal seat,
Calls, "Lady! Sunny! Step up!" And they do.
They know their names as well as we know ours.
Behind, the earth unzips its sleeping bag
And looks around, turns over with a thump,
Tucks in its head and settles back to sleep.
Ahead, that tall white mare beyond the hills
Looks out to see them shouldering their work,
Reciting sonnets as they go along.
I look real hard, then quickly close my eyes
To capture one bright picture from this time
When two big horses make a lovely rhyme.

The Purple Hat

There once was a lady
    Who wore a felt hat
That was purple as grape juice
    And soft as a cat.

She wore it with dresses,
    She wore it with pants,
Yes, she wore it to dine in,
    She wore it to dance.

She wore it to bed,
    And she wore it to shower;
She wouldn't remove it
    Whatever the hour.

This lady was weeding
    Her garden one day
When her dog grabbed that hat—
    Yes, he snatched it away.

He nabbed that old hat thingy
    Right off her head,
And he took off across
    Her new vegetable bed.

The lady leaped up
    And she screeched like a cat,
And she chased that dog thief
    And got hold of her hat.

That dog, he was big,
 Yes, that dog, he was strong,
And he had some white teeth
 About nine inches long.

He wouldn't let go of it,
 Neither would she;
Oh, they tugged and they wrassled
 From two until three.

The dog, he was growling;
 The lady, she swore;
Oh, they made a big racket
 From three until four.

They stepped on some pansies,
 They went round the shed,
And they jumped all the vines
 In the cucumber bed.

They trampled some daisies,
 They knocked down some figs,
And they slipped in the mud
 And got dirty as pigs.

No matter what happened,
 Up high or down low,
They just wouldn't give up,
 They just wouldn't let go.

(cont'd)

They bumped on the bird bath,
    Got scratched by a rose,
They were slapped by a shrub,
    Then they tripped on the hose.

They fell in the hammock,
    Both lady and hound,
And it flipped up and dumped them
    Right out on the ground.

At last that old hat
    Couldn't take any more.
That old purple hat ripped.
    That old purple hat tore.

It ripped right apart
    From the crown to the brim,
And a half went to her,
    And a half went to him.

They both of them landed
    Smack dab on their rumps,
And the hat parts went flying
    And fell in two lumps.

The lady was crying,
    The dog pawed and whined,
And the hat was in two hunks,
    One fore and one hind.

The lady got up
    And she looked at her hat.
Well, it sure was a sight.
    And yet that was not that.

She wiped off her tears
    On the front of her shirt.
Then she picked up the pieces
    And shook off the dirt.

She took them inside
    And she turned on the light.
Then she fit them together
    Until they looked right.

She got out a needle.
    She got out some thread.
Then she popped on her thimble.
    "I'll fix it," she said.

She sewed up that hat.
    She was sure she could do it.
She stitched it together
    And said, "Nothing to it!"

She found a big ribbon,
    A lovely lime green,
And she tied on a bow
    That was fit for a queen.

(cont'd)

She sewed it in place.
    Then she tried on her hat.
Then she looked in the mirror
    And gave it a pat.

And that purple hat
    Is still snug on her head,
And she don't give a rip
    For what anyone's said.

She wears it with dresses,
    She wears it with pants,
Yes, she wears it to dine in,
    She wears it to dance.

She wears it to bed,
    And she wears it to shower;
She still won't remove it,
    Whatever the hour.

But there's just one place
    Where she doesn't dare wear it,
And that's in her garden.
    Her dog, he can't bear it!

Sometimes that old dog,
    As he sleeps on the floor,
Is a-twitch as he dreams
    Of the purple-hat war!

It's A Good Day

So first we ran out of milk,
And someone said they hated oatmeal,
And then the cat made it known that it had to be let out
    instantly,
And someone couldn't find their second sock, without which
    life would be insupportable for another moment,
And a bowl filled with oatmeal and peaches and cream and
    honey all carefully and artistically arranged just so got
    accidentally dropped on the floor,
And then the phone rang, which it never rings at this time
    of day,
And someone raced through the kitchen dragging a belt with
    all three kittens chasing it,
And the person who had been planning to wear the belt ran
    through chasing *them*,
And it just so happened that there was a huge spider in the
    bathtub,
And what's more, we were fresh out of toilet paper to kill
    it with,
And the parakeet was not supposed to be let out of its cage
    right now,
Although maybe it could eat the spider,
And does anybody know how that oatmeal got up on the
    ceiling?
But all in all, I'll say this for it:
It was a good day,
Really, it was a very good day,
Which I know because when I went to put on my coat and go
    get the mail,
I was able to say (unlike yesterday),
You know it's a good day when there's no dead mouse
    in your boot!

Zephyr

I waited where a path went up a bank,
Around a boulder, up into the green;
The air was the best wine I ever drank,
As morning raised the curtain on the scene;
Above, a robin, pleasingly rotund,
Was harvesting some lichen for its nest,
While jays pretended, imitated, punned,
And sober sparrows fell for every jest;
I waited, and I saw a fern-seed wind
Come down the path, glad-handing all the plants;
It glided up and kissed me, then it grinned
And vanished, while my heart kept up the dance...
    These small epiphanies were anti-gray
    And luminized an ordinary day.

Rose Window

The frozen juice is brought out from the household antarctic—
Plunked down on the counter—
The metal lid is polar-capped with frost—
The plastic strip stubborn, skink-tailed,
Requiring the pliers to be gotten out—
Taste—
This orange juice has been lifting weights,
Must be the only thing in the store
Not already watered down—
Orange sludge is crowbarred with a butter knife,
Dump-slumped into the pitcher—
As the water rivers from the faucet,
Orange foam beers up—
Stirred according to an old recipe
That specifies beating for so many minutes
While holding only good thoughts—
The orange bubbles assemble in the middle,
Celled together as if by bees—
Ease the big spoon out—
One full-blown rose, spinning, slowing,
Silent with inner beauty—
Still slowly rotating
As it is borne to the table
To be poured out.

Penstemonium

The cut-leaf penstemons grow thick in pots;
The buds crowd up the stems in eager ranks,
Some nothing more than tiny yellow dots,
Some little fish with scarlet on their flanks,
Some bigger fish with haughty mouths shut tight—
And all the biggest ones begin to sing:
Their splendid soft magenta throats are bright
With buzzing black and yellow notes that zing
From mouth to mouth like catchy little tunes;
And when the songs are done, the fishes fall;
They slip their stems until the porch is strewn
With purple dresses for a fairy's doll...
   One bee goes in a likely-looking bloom
   And both fall with a thump! and one goes zoom!

Sky Writing

The sky all morning was completely blue,
As smooth and empty as a blank new page,
Till after lunch some clouds came drifting through,
Like poems written by a playful sage
About the feathers swallows use for catch,
The fluff the wind puffs out from cottonwoods,
The smoke that spirals from a blown-out match,
The soft sweet curls that halo toddlers' hoods;
All afternoon, above the shining pines,
The sky's been slowly, silently inscrolled
With luminous illuminated lines
That dreamers lying on the grass behold:
    The ruminations of late summertime
    Have now condensed into loquacious rhyme.

Change

Fall has been lying around,
golden and beautiful,
like a mountain lion sprawled out full and lazy.

Then one morning,
instead of kicking off its blankets first thing,
the sun decides to sleep in.
The wind throws down a book it has been reading about
    civilization
and says it is bored.
It gets restless, then playful,
then mischievous, then ornery.
The mountain lion folds its ears sideways,
gets up, and slips away.

And the needles begin to fall.
All through the long blustery afternoon,
the ponderosas release their needles,
the oldest ones,
which they have spent these last few weeks
carefully drying and dyeing a pale orangey-tan
that sometimes, if your eyes are blurred or in a hurry,
turns to an astonishing pink
against the bright blue sky.
In the wild wind,
the pines run their fingers through their hair
and comb out these sunrise needles

and strew them on the banqueting floor below,
fragrant, crisp, prickly,
until everything is graciously covered:
the bare compacted places,
the tired grass, the gravel driveway,
the dropped scraps and the collapsed weeds;
all now strewn over and ready for dancing,
or for putting up a tipi and spreading some trade blankets.

The next morning, the trees stand around,
completely green again,
pleased with the earth's new look,
done just in time for this cold fresh new day.

The Surprise

All evening it was raining pretty hard.
Outside, the dancing water soaked the porch,
The primrose pots and tubs of tulip buds.
The Frisbee upside down beside the path
Had turned into a little dolly pool.
The dirt was gleaming mud, all squish and squelch,
And everything was wet and cold and dark,
And every tree trunk, every blade of grass,
Was touched with rainbow colors on one side,
Reflections of the Christmas strings left up
To cheer late-winter evenings till spring comes,
And every raindrop was a spear of light.
Inside, the lamps glowed yellow by the fire,
The food was good and hot, and yes, it's true,
It's been too dry, the land sure needs the rain.
And so put down our books, and so to bed.
Outside, the drums and dancing carried on
Long after everyone was fast asleep,
Till sometime in the middle of the night
The rain tribe finished their emphatic dance
And put away their drums, and changed their clothes
To robes of soft white fur, and turned to snow.
And quietly they danced around the yard
With fans of soft white feathers in their hands,
And every dark thing slowly turned to white,
While in the house the sleepers softly slept.
By morning it was three-four inches deep.
"Oh, look! It snowed! I never thought it would!"
Up quick, and hurry into boots and coats!
Outside, the snow was full of polished flakes

That sparkled in the sun between the trees
And fluffed up in the air when snow was kicked,
And soon the yard was full of happy tracks
That squeaked when they were made, and stuck to boots,
And looked like snow-white buckskin. On the porch,
The primrose faces and the tulip heads—
Bright yellow, purple, cherry red, rich pink—
Were glowing under fluffy snow-white wigs,
Their leaves a vibrant green, all topped with snow.
By lunch, the snow had soaked into the dirt
And reached the roots of all the sleeping plants.
It won't be long now till the big spring dance.

The Last Walkabout

Just time for one more journey round the yard,
One little trip to visit all these friends.
Right here, beside the steps up to the door,
The lady's-eardrops dangle thick and bright;
And now the small azalea's solid green,
Its last few flowers fallen in the grass,
Pink dresses for a stick used as a doll.
The buds are thick along this little bush
Whose name we have not figured out just yet.
And here's the tree where bushtits come to roost,
Green in the leaves, like little leaves themselves,
And sing their tiny songs and settle down,
While God pokes at his campfire in the west.
And this camellia, old as this old house,
Chopped down to just a stump before we came,
Now vigorously springing up again,
Its leaves as bright as patent-leather shoes:
We hoped it would become a tree once more.
Beneath this window here, from which we saw
A bald eagle the day that we moved in,
A little yellow poppy blooms each year,
Dependent on our thoughtful disregard.
Some buds have come out on the columbines
And on the exuberant pot marigolds.
Looks like the chives are doing pretty well,
And, hey, the parsley's finally come up—
Up just in time to greet us as we go—
For go we must, or pay a bigger rent

Than we can cut from our small monthly pie.
Yes, Money once again takes up its scythe,
And throws a roast to Conscience on its chain,
And comes to cut down all our fine new growth.
Oh, we're just cuttings, oh, to tell the truth,
We're really cuttings of cuttings of cuttings,
Afflicted with the virus of despair
Which now we'll have to outgrow once again.

Requiem For A Mobile Home

How hollow
Inside me
Is the hole
This house once filled,
A home-shaped place
At the hub of the world.

No—don't explain—
Don't try to tell
What particular logic
The landlord mouths,
What cold-eyed god
He invokes.

No—don't ask me
To wish him ill;
That's one load
I don't have to box up
And cart away.

No—I won't stay
To see this soft space
Under the archway
Where we so often stood together,
This well-known pattern
Of moving shade
Where we so often sat together,

Destroyed by someone
Hard with lawfulness,
Armed with dollar signs.

May this junky little house,
This shabby little porch,
Glow with the memory
Of how very much we loved it
Even while it is being torn down.

Flagging

When I see that flag flying over the dam,
So huge that it has its own tidal waves,
I wish so much that I could be proud of my country.

The Indigenous Renter

Now people have cut Mother Earth up into squares,
And they buy and sell those squares
As if Mother Earth is nothing but a whore.
I guess eloquence is in vain.
If you so much as dare to enjoy the sparkle
On someone else's water,
You're trespassing—
Yes, they've made it a crime—
A crime that even Jesus has committed—
Jesus, the ultimate homeless person,
With nowhere to lay his head.
People treat each other worse than animals.
No one evicts birds from their nests
For not paying rent,
But us naked two-legged creatures
With heads the right shape for crowns
Are not allowed to have a place at Mother Earth's breast
Without first paying for it
And shoving someone else off the nipple.

When will everyone be able to sit quietly
On the dirt inside their own tipi?

Trespassing

I crossed a fence where it lay on a bank;
Two mossy posts had died some time ago;
On one, a lichened plywood square, now blank.
The sun had melted off the recent snow;
The grass was wide and empty in the breeze;
A stream with lots to say went down the vale
Between the feet of voluble old trees.
I leaped this dolly river to a trail
That topped a knoll where oaks grew tall and stout,
And there I leaned against a pendent limb,
The wind fresh in my face, the view spread out
From green to blue to lavender to dim...
    I crossed the fence, as lawless as a bear,
    And stole the thing of greatest value there.

The Mountain Man (Heart-Leaf Buckwheat, *Eriogonum compositum*)

I wear a paradox for clothes,
As soft as any kitten's nose,
Yet tough as twenty buffaloes (as long as they don't charge).

I made a bow, I tracked a deer,
I dried the meat for winter cheer,
I tanned the hide from tail to ear and made myself a shirt.

I've paid exactly what it cost,
No one exploited, no one bossed,
And no one's habitat is lost, though mine is not too large.

Some think my smell is not so nice,
But life has got an earthy spice,
And though this sure ain't paradise, I love my share of dirt.

Tree Dance

Ponderosa's dance clothes
Are richly tessellated brocade
Elaborately fringed
Haloed with insect-wing lace
Squirrel-scalloped
Topped with a bird-wing headdress
She sings when she dances
A song so old the words are lost
Her sisters join in
And they dance night into day

To David Attenborough

Perhaps it's the way you're willing
to ride an elephant anywhere,
or the way you're always putting on
a new kind of helmet...

Perhaps it's the way you tell us
about the straightforward paws,
the little muddy nest,
the trace of nourishing dust...

Perhaps it's the way you let that seabird
take off from your shoulders,
or the way you dig fast
so that we too can see the golden mole...

Perhaps it's the smile you have
for that little black and white bird...

Perhaps.
Or perhaps for sheer joy.

An Inordinate Fondness

When God does the beetles,
They line up at the door of his workshop,
All a plain unfinished buffy color.
The line snakes away into the distance.
God calls, "Okay, ready!"
And the first one goes in and climbs up on God's workbench.
God has his cuffs rolled up above his elbows
And his long white hair tied back in a ponytail.
He adjusts his magnifier,
Says, "Now then, hold real still,"
And takes up a small tool
With which he delicately carves row after row of tiny dots
On the beetle's elongated back.
Then he pushes the magnifier away,
And with a bit of sponge
He paints a subtle all-over camouflage pattern
In ashy gray, dark brown, soft black.
Gently God blows on the beetle to dry it.
Then it crawls to the open window,
Lifts its newly limned wing cases,
Spreads its splendid lucid wings,
Begins to buzz and at the same time
Releases its claw-hold on the window frame
And launches forth,
Out through the wonderful transparent air
To the brown and green world below.
When God has seen it well on its way,
He calls again, "Okay, ready!"
And the next little creature comes, a small round domed one.
It turns this way and that
As God carefully paints its legs and body black.
He takes up an old brush that has just a few hairs

And adds some touches of pure white.
He chooses bright red for the wing cases.
He pauses, hand hovering,
Then dips a small round brush into the black paint
And gently dots it onto the red.
God has used quick-drying paint,
And as soon as the wing cases are ready,
He waxes and polishes them
Until this three-part animal shines like a jewel.
At last it too is done and flies away,
Elytra opened like pocket-watch covers,
Wings a blurred fan of exhilaration.
The next one, a small straight-sided oval, comes
And is neatly painted a shiny iridescent green all over.
And so it goes all day long.
One after another the beetles get fixed up,
Each one different,
And set out to seek their fortunes.
When the last one has gone,
God leans back,
Stretching luxuriantly and yawning.
"Well, *that* was fun," he says.
Slowly he puts everything away,
Cleaning and lining up his tools,
Capping his paints,
Washing and pointing his brushes,
Scraping his palette.
He scrubs the paint off his hands.
He undoes his ponytail and shakes out his hair.
Then he goes off to get a little supper,
And someone says, "How many beetles?"
And God just shrugs and smiles, and says, "God alone knows."

At The Christmas Concert

The choir painted their clothes inky black
And their music brilliant white.
The violinist made friction sing.
The fingers of the pianist were like a herd of deer
Bounding over wet rocks in a snowy field.
The eyes of the soloist shone like stars,
And round golden notes soared out of her mouth
And melted on us like butter on toast.
And if only they had used colored smoke in the pipe organ!
We drank in the music like water.
We clapped like wild horses galloping.
And at the end,
We all sang the anthem like a host of angels.
For that one moment, we were all radiant together.
When it was over,
Some of us hurried out of the auditorium,
Praising God for flush toilets.

The Textile Artist (Yarrow, *Achillea millefolium*)

I used to keep my people warm
In frost and wind and fog and storm;
With bits of fluff and sticks I formed the magic stuff of clothes.

My spindle spun with giddy cheer,
My needles fenced like eager deer,
And loop by tiny loop appeared the missing human pelt.

Sometimes a child would come to see
How much was done, whose it would be,
And questing fingers gently squeezed the springy finished rows.

Well, times have changed, but I'm still true;
I do things no machine can do;
I could still save your life if you will let the spell be felt.

In Will's Garden

Not that it's what he would have planted,
Nor even that he would have liked it here,

But just that I keep getting reminded of him
By so many things:

The bean seeds with their substantial doublets
And their little codpieces;

The twin pea pods hanging from the same node,
Indistinguishable brother and sister;

The heavy-headed sunflowers
Contemplating the tragic earth;

The mischievous chickweed
Transforming the garden overnight;

The stakes topped with upside-down seed packets
Like so many sucket forks lifting so many morsels;

The thatched O in the unpruned grapes
Where the robin broods;

The faded parchment leaf on the path
Under my cross-gartered high-tops;

The heap of greenery masking the pitchfork's burnished spears
As I march toward the compost pile;

The hollow ball of white string unrolling as it is passed up
    and down
In a fine frenzy to string the trellis;

The seven stages of the well-grown tomato
From eager seed to fall-felled tangle;

The heavy glove abruptly thrown down
For the sake of the poppy's flocked heart;

The midnight gopher underneath it all
Intent on revenge;

The flowers so sweetly mothering
Whatever tiny creature comes;

The grasshoppers with their enthusiastic wings
Applauding all entrances and exits...

I can see Will now, sitting on an upturned bucket
Next to the faucet, scribbling like crazy.

Beau Leopard

One day I met a leopard who'd
    Been up for most the night.
He said, "I haven't slepard, I
    Suppose I look a fright!"

And then he wailed and wepard, "Oh,
    I've hunted till I'm sore!
I've crawled and creeped and crepard, but
The prey's been so obstrepard! Why,
I feel almost decrepard! It
    Is such a dreadful bore!"

A silly prey then stepard out,
    Right out into the clear.
It put itself in jeopard. It
Was totally inepard. I
Propounded, quipped, and quepard, "What's
    It think it's doing here?"

That leopard was no shepherd. He
    Was really out for blood.
That hungry leopard lepard—but
The prey was quite intrepard, and
    It rolled into the mud.

The leopard turned quite tepard when
    Its prey behaved so crass.
It said, "I'm not too hepard on
A prey that's not been swepard. I
    Suppose I'll take a pass."

This tale is lightly peppered with
    A moral that rings true:
The sillier a leopard gets,
The more a prey's incepard wits
Get sharpened to decepard tricks
To give a picky leopard yicks
    Instead of being stew.

Indian Paintbrush

I know what House Finch uses
to paint his face
for the big spring dance.

In Which A Native-Plant Enthusiast Surprises Us By Her Choice Of Favorite Plant

Now this here is a noxious weed.
You gotta pull it up real quick
Before it sets some noxious seed.
Make sure your gloves are good and thick
Because it's full of prickly "ows,"
And sticky sap drips down its stalks.
What's more, it kills both sheep and cows,
And smells like skunks in dirty socks.
It's armored, bristled, thorned, and spined.
I love this plant. I think it's great,
In such a mixed-up world, to find
A thing that it's okay to hate.

Obituary

Oh, the sky is so empty
Where your tree once stood.
So short a time ago,
This pale blue space was full
Of branches rich with life,
A strong old trunk,
A still-growing top.
And now it's empty sky.
Just so empty.

The little birds that used to fly
Back and forth from my tree to yours
Are circling in this emptiness,
Calling their high thin cries,
Sharp as knives.
They return to me with empty beaks
And it begins to rain again.

I truly cannot believe
That there is only dust.
Where are you now?
I send my birds out again
And they vanish.

I am still waiting here
For one of them to return
With some kind of leaf in its beak.

On Planet Earth

What is this strange place?
Hurricanes, those giant cyclops,
Harriers with their dripping claws,
Hirsute red-eyed beasts,
Hyphae insidious and invidious,
Herod with his bloody hands...
Oh, the horror!
In this strange place,
Herbs curl up and blacken;
Hummingbirds falter and fall to earth;
Health turns to hell;
Hapless creatures hunt for help,
Unrolling their desperate tracks;
The continents are ripped apart and reeling.
Oh, this strange hard terrible place!

Yet the sun keeps shining on all this wretchedness.
Somewhere, the merciful rain is falling
To wash the rocks and soak into the dust.
The gentle grass is coming
To transform the barren hills.
Seeds sprout among the bones.
That doe with one useless hind leg
Suddenly shows up with twin fawns.
Someone pushes that heavy little box to the back of the shelf,
Turns and flings open a case,
Strikes bird-voiced sparks with horsehair and steel strings,
Brings that hollow wooden heart to life once more.

What *is* this strange hard terrible amazing place?

Uninvited

My soul came to the door the other day,
Along about dusk. "How's it going, Soul?"
I said as I let it in. "It's been a long time."

"Too long," said my soul. "Got a bite to eat?"
I thought my soul didn't look too good:
Scrawny, dirty, dressed in rags, shivering a little.

It took a seat by the fire and held out its hands to the blaze.
I got out some leftovers, and it wolfed everything down.
"I'm still hungry," it said. "You don't change much," I said.

"You're doing well, by the looks of it," said my soul.
"Not too bad," I said, trying to be modest,
"Keeping the wolf from the door, at any rate."

"How about putting me up for a while?" said my soul.
"I don't have any room," I said quickly. "I have guests coming.
The kids wouldn't like it. Don't look at me like that!"

My soul has the kind of eyes that can see right through you.
"I've been sleeping under bridges," it said. "In haystacks.
I've been living off crumbs, scraps, garbage!"

"I don't want you here!" I said. "You know we don't get along!
You're never willing to compromise.
With you, it's always one big fight!"

"I don't believe in compromise!" said my soul.
It started to get that wild look.
Suddenly it jumped up and took off its coat,

Or what passed for a coat, anyway,
Some old rag I wouldn't be caught dead in.
It threw off its hat. It kicked off its shoes.

Then it actually began ripping off its shirt.
"You stop that right now!" I yelled.
"Do you think I want to see you naked?"

"This isn't about you," said my soul. "It's about me.
I'm tired of hiding. I'm tired of disguises.
I'm sick to death of everything!"

"Why do you have to come here and make a scene?" I cried.
"I don't need this kind of grief!
You're going to ruin everything!"

Now the only thing my soul was wearing
Was some kind of plaid thing wrapped around like a skirt.
It ripped this off, too. I turned my back.

"I want you to get out!" I yelled. "Now!"
My soul ignored me. It looked around,
Then went over and pulled a blanket off the wall,

(cont'd)

Not any old blanket but my best Indian blanket,
The prize of my collection of genuine pre-white artifacts,
Irreplaceable. "Put that back!" I shouted.

My soul wrapped this around itself like in a painting.
It stood there looking at me in that way it has.
"What's got into you?" I howled. My soul said, "Got a peace
    pipe?"

Well, I wasn't about to let it wreck any more of my treasures.
So it went to the garage and helped itself to my tools.
It said it would make what it needed.

Now it's morning and my soul is still here.
It's out back, building some kind of a lodge, I guess,
Stubborn as a pig. What on earth next, I wonder.

Armed

I will fight the thing that says no.
I will fight it with flowers
And with my footsteps
And with this beautiful little stone.

The thing that says no
At all the wrong times
And never says yes, ever,
I will fight with this little song I have made up
And this little plant I am watering.
I will get my broom and dustpan
And fight again.

I will contemplate this tree growing straight
And this tree growing like a dancer.
I will take a drink of fresh water,
Hitch up my jeans,
And fight the thing that says no.

I will fail again and again.
But I will fight.
And I will find the path.

White Things

The gentle gibbous moon
Is an oval portrait of itself in soft focus,
Exposing the hidden mistiness in the air,
Hanging on the faded pale-gray wallpaper sky;
It is a luminous white balloon
Floating fearlessly above the jagged outline of the cliff,
Above the ponderosas bristling with porcupine hands...

The paper birches, several trunks densely clumped,
Have flung off their old yellow jackets
And do their stretches in white clothes,
Snow-white, but showing just a touch, a hint,
Of their warm underbark in one or two places;
Their white arms reach up and out,
Graceful above the old gray boulders
Circle-wagoned around them
By some yard-maker with a big machine...

A lavish crop of snowberries, brave and bright,
Spangles the dull twigs of a big bush,
Shining among the scruffy leftover leaves
Like drops of fresh white paint;
They hang by ones, by twos, by severals,
Fat and lovely ornaments
Above the dark ivy on the dark stones...

Here on Earth's rotating breast,
The slowly deepening colors sink
Into ever more tenebrious tones,
The tan to burnt umber,
The gray to somber murk,
The green to nearly black,
As night gets mixed into every color on the palette...

Except the white things.
For a while in the twilight,
They seem to give off light instead of slurp it up.
Nothing stains their beauty.
No matter who is not looking,
They remain true to their whiteness,
A prayer for those of us with divided hearts.

Were I A Cow

To stand, ruminant in the starlight,
While whole stories of odors flow past,
Calmly holding my own heat, warm in the cool air,
My strong feet foursquare on the firm dirt,
My body aligned with the mysterious magnetic forces of
    the earth...

To graze with softly whiskered half-moon lips
More sensitive than fingers,
Searching through every vegetable refinement,
Gathering the sacrificial grass, the gentle forbs,
Taking pleasure in the mastery of this vital task
Without which there would be no cows...

To lay down on the faithful ground,
Legs neatly folded in satisfying patterns,
And thoughtfully begin the long unhurried meditations of the cud,
Like a sage in contemplation of a proverb
That reveals more and more meaning
The longer it is savored...

To give voice:
To moo the most resplendent, dark, compelling moo,
A potent wordless call that shivers all the leaves,
And rings across the field, and bells out into the hills,
And lifts the heart of every kindred creature...

Were I a cow.

The Percussionist (Wild Rose In Fall)

Musicians lift horns, reeds, and bows;
I stand behind the curving rows;
We're waiting here in eager pose to put a concert on.

My drumsticks hover like a pair
Of keen antennae in the air;
The audience goes still at their compelling magic charm.

This silent moment, charged with power,
Will open like a time-lapse flower
At that first downward move of our conductor's raised baton.

I've practiced cadence, lilt, and din,
And now I'm hoping once again
The bird of music will fly in and land here on my arm.

Drumming

God is out on the hills, drumming.
He has found a nice big long chunk of hollow oak in the woodpile
And split off all the bark, and carved the inside smooth,
And stretched some rawhide over one end,
And gone out to see what he can do with it.
He is out there now, sitting on a rock
in the dappled shade of an oak tree,
drumming softly with his hands.
Out of the secret woods
flies a pair of downy woodpeckers.
They land on a nearby tree,
and look, and listen, and hitch up the trunk a bit,
and join in the drumming.
Then a red-shafted flicker comes,
watches with a bright eye,
finds a resonant dead branch,
and joins in, too.
Then some nuthatches come,
both red- and white-breasted,
working down the trunks with staccato beaks.
Then a big pileated woodpecker comes,
flaring his red crest,
and starts excavating a snag in perfect rhythm.
All around, the crickets begin chirping,
and the fence lizards come through the bushes
in fits and starts
and climb up on the rocks

and do little push-ups,
flashing their blue undersides.
And the click beetles come,
snapping and turning aerial somersaults around God's ankles.
One little woodpecker even flies down
to the side of God's drum.
Everyone is drumming, louder, stronger, fuller, brighter,
drumming out a tapestry, a laminated cadence,
until the very marrows of the trees begin to beat,
and the half-buried rocks fairly resonate;
yes, everyone is drumming up a gradual crescendo,
slowly increasing, greatening,
growing together to the final bright triumphant stroke—Hey!
Then
For one moment
Everyone is silent in unison.
And then God grins and says, "Hey, everyone, that was great!"

Praetorius

Hey, they're playing your music on the radio!
The brocade notes vibrate out into the living room
With its worn-out second-hand couch and its ugly lamps.

A whole raft of recorders chirps like a flock of birds in
    a willow tree,
A harpsichord twinkles like sunlight on a rippling stream,
A cello hums thoughtfully,
A lute is confidently plucked.
Some kind of little drum teases our feet
To start tapping out imagined antique dance steps
That require those shoes with long pointy toes curled up
Or an elegant velvet skirt,
And every now and then a tiny bell waves its magic wand over
    the notes.

Yes, the music blooms today in this modern living room
Like a wildflower reproducing itself unchanged
Despite its passage through the years,
As fresh as when it bloomed for you hundreds of years ago,
The first time musicians breathed life into it.

Everything else from that day is lost:
The smell of the air in the building,
The quality of the light sliding along the violin bows,
The dance everyone actually did,
What they said about your new music,
The interplay of unrecorded manners, or the lack of manners,
The ephemeral slang,
The little jokes of the moment, if people let themselves joke,

What was served for dinner,
How they really felt about the luxury of power
And the sea of peasants out there...

Everything is lost but the music,
Which is still as fresh in this reincarnation as it ever was,
Seeding itself into the future
For as long as there are musicians
Who can play the sackbut.

Now that hilarious crumhorn joins in
Like a giant bumblebee holding its nose,
Inviting us to jump up from the couch,
Usurp the noble privilege,
Prance around the coffee table in those pointy shoes,
Really make that velvet skirt fly.

The Renegade Biologist (Yellow Bells, *Fritillaria pudica*)

When morning stains the folded hills,
When evening fades from rose to chills,
I lift my lantern high to kill the darkness on my way.

While shadows rotate round the trees,
While bats team-rope the prowling breeze,
I hold my lantern out to ease some light on wary things.

What seems so clear is none too bright,
And what's obscure is not just night;
And that's why I use lantern light by darkness and by day.

This burning curiosity—
These questions spawning endlessly—
If facts enough lay eggs, I'll see the truth hatch out with wings.

The Optimist (Pot Marigold,
Calendula officinalis)

Some people say there should be gloomth
When there's so often news of doomth;
I've got some nerve, producing bloomth when everything's
    so bad.

But I'm not ever gonna be
A dark-side ponderosity:
I gotta work on settin' seed, or more bad news gets done.

Yes, I've still got a source of warmth;
To soak up light and grow is normth,
To put out leaves and weather stormth, and bloom and bloom
    like mad.

So when the prospect gets too gray,
More color's what we need, I say;
I'm gonna keep on with the play that leads me to the sun.

The End

Index Of Titles And First Lines

Colophon

The text of this book was prepared using the open-source software Linux and LibreOffice, and the open-source typefaces Bookman (for the title pages) and Liberation (for all else).

35944715R00095

Made in the USA
San Bernardino, CA
09 July 2016

"...I tell you here and now
That it's okay to be alive
And make a path through the grass."

ISBN 9781512118193

9000

9 781512 118193